# HOT DESERTS

Rose Pipes

A ZOË BOOK

## A ZOË BOOK

© 1997 Zoë Books Limited

Devised and produced by
Zoë Books Limited
15 Worthy Lane
Winchester
Hampshire SO23 7AB
England

First published in Great Britain in 1997 by
Zoë Books Limited
15 Worthy Lane
Winchester
Hampshire SO23 7AB

A record of the CIP data is available from the British
Library.

ISBN 1 86173 015 2

Printed in Italy by Grafedit SpA
Editor: Kath Davies
Map: Sterling Associates
Design & Production: Sterling Associates

## Photographic acknowledgments

The publishers wish to acknowledge, with thanks,
the following photographic sources:

Robert Harding Picture Library 16; The Hutchison
Library / Angela Silvertop - title page; / Wilkinson
5; Impact Photos / Alan Keohane 9, 18, 20; / John
Evans 12; / Bruce Stephens 21; NHPA / Anthony
Bannister 8; / Dan Griggs 15; / Lady Philippa
Scott 19; ANT/Bill Bachman 25; South American
Pictures / Tony Morrison 26, 29 / Robert Francis
28; Still Pictures / T de Salis - cover background; /
Klein/Hubert - cover inset bl; / M & C Denis-Huot
4; / J.P.Delobelle 7; / John Newby 11; / Werner
Gartung 13; / Christian Testu 27; TRIP / Eric
Smith 23; Woodfall Wild Images / Adrian Dorst
17; / Ted Mead 22; Zefa - cover inset tr, 10, 14,
24.

The publishers have made every effort to trace the
copyright holders, but if they have inadvertently
overlooked any, they will be pleased to make the
necessary arrangement at the first opportunity.

# Contents

# What are hot deserts?

Deserts are very dry places. Rain may not fall there for months, or even years. Deserts may be sandy or stony, flat or mountainous.

In this picture of a desert in Algeria, you can see rocks as well as sand. The big waves, or ripples, in the sand are called **sand dunes**.

In the daytime, a hot desert may be 40°C in the shade. But even the hottest deserts can be cold at night. In winter, frost may lie on the ground in the early morning.

Deserts are windy places. Strong winds blow up thick dust or **sand storms** that can last for days.

A sand storm in Africa

# Where are the hot deserts?

The biggest hot desert is the Sahara, in Africa. This desert is almost as big as the United States of America.

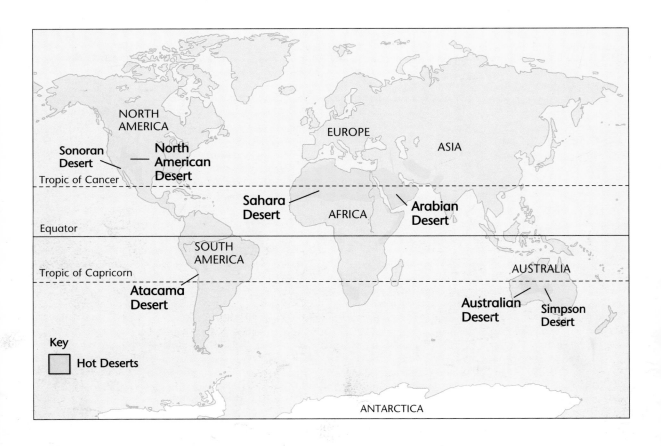

This map shows the world's hot deserts. The hottest deserts are close to the **Tropics**.

Wind and water make some of the shapes we see in deserts. Heavy rain carries away sand, stones and rocks, and makes deep gashes in the ground. Rivers, too, cut down into the desert rocks to make deep **canyons**.

Strong winds blow sand and stones against the rocks to carve out strange shapes.

These rocks are in Utah in the USA.

# Desert animals and plants

In desert **habitats**, many animals burrow underground to keep cool.

The camel stores food in its hump, and can live for days without water. Its large feet stop it from sinking into soft sand, and its long eye-lashes keep sand out of its eyes.

Some plants store water in their stems or leaves, or grow long roots to reach down to underground water. They have **adapted** to desert life.

There is water in the desert at an **oasis**, either in pools or under the ground. People come here with their animals for water, food and to buy and sell goods. Farmers can grow crops here.

This oasis is in southern Morocco, Africa.

# The Sahara Desert in Africa

The Sahara Desert crosses twelve countries in north Africa.

Much of the Sahara is stony and there are some mountains. In the sandy parts, the wind blows the sand into small ripples and tall dunes.

No plants grow in parts of the Sahara. There, animals hunt other creatures for food. Many animals hunt at night when it is coolest.

The Fennec fox lives in burrows. Its large feet stop it from sinking into sand, and its fur keeps it warm on cold nights.

The Fennec fox has large ears which help it to stay cool. It can hear sounds up to a kilometre away.

There are salt mines in the Sahara Desert. The Tuareg people of the Sahara have been salt **traders** for hundreds of years.

The Tuareg carry the blocks of salt across the desert on camels. The salt shown here came from Taoudenni in Mali.

When oil was found in the Sahara, desert life changed. People moved in to drill oil wells. There are new roads and airports because of the oil trade. Tourists can use them to visit the desert.

Oil workers move around the desert in cars and trucks. Here they are checking an oil well in Tunisia.

The Tuareg people guide tourists through the desert. They also make money by hiring out camels to tourists.

# The Sonoran Desert in North America

The Sonoran is the biggest desert in North America. It is famous for its cactus plants.

The saguaro cactus grows up to 15 metres high and can live for 200 years. Cacti take in water through their roots, and store it in their thick, waxy stems.

The cacti and other plants that grow there are adapted to heat, cold and dryness.

Many desert animals need cacti to live. The pronghorn antelope eats the flesh of the prickly pear cactus. Birds and insects also eat cactus fruits.

Bees and long-nosed bats drink **nectar** from cactus flowers.

This Gila woodpecker nests in a saguaro cactus. When the woodpecker leaves, other birds will move in.

The Sonoran Desert is cold in winter and very hot in summer. It is also very dry and dusty.

Highways link towns and cities in the Sonoran Desert. The largest city is Phoenix, the State capital of Arizona. You can see it in this picture.

Phoenix gets its water from underground and from rivers. Water for farmland comes from the Colorado River, which is 541 kilometres away. The river water is carried in pipelines, channels and tunnels.

Farmers often use mules to move around the desert.

# The Arabian Desert

The Arabian Desert lies between the Red Sea and the Persian Gulf. Part of this desert is called the Empty Quarter.

The Empty Quarter is as big as France. It is mostly sand dunes, like those in this picture. In summer, it is too hot for people to live here.

The sand gazelle lives in the Arabian Desert. It eats the leaves of desert plants for food and water.

Many gazelles died because sheep and goats ate their food, and because people hunted them. Today, there are desert **wildlife reserves**, where gazelles and other creatures have food to eat, and are safe from hunters.

This sand gazelle is searching for food.

The Bedouin people were once **nomads**. They moved their sheep and goats around the desert to find food and water.

Today, most Bedouin live and work in towns near the coast. Some people still keep animals in the desert. Most of them use trucks, not camels, to travel around.

There is oil under the desert and the Persian Gulf. This oil has made the Arabian Desert countries very rich.

Many desert towns and cities have fine new buildings, parks and lakes. It costs a lot of money to provide water for the plants, lakes and fountains.

The city of Abu Dhabi near the Persian Gulf.

# The Simpson Desert in Australia

Desert covers nearly half the **continent** of Australia. The driest part is near the centre and is called the Simpson Desert.

This is Chambers Rock in the Simpson Desert.

Rain may not fall in this desert for years. It is an empty place, with no towns or farms.

The Simpson Desert is famous for its long, straight sand dunes. Some of these dunes are as long as 220 kilometres.

This picture of the dunes was taken from an aircraft.

More than 230 kinds of lizard live in Australia. The 'thorny devil' lives in the desert. It eats up to 5000 insects a day!

The thorny devil has adapted to dry places. Its folded skin traps tiny drops of water, which run down the folds into the lizard's mouth. This may be all it drinks for months, or even years.

At the southern end of the Simpson Desert is Lake Eyre. It is the largest lake in Australia. In most years, there is no water in the lake, only glittering white salt.

If it rains heavily, Lake Eyre fills with water. Thousands of birds arrive when the lake is full.

Australasian pelicans at Lake Eyre

# The Atacama Desert in South America

The Atacama is the driest desert in the world. In some parts of the Atacama, rain has not fallen for more than a hundred years.

The desert lies between the Andes Mountains and the Pacific Ocean in northern Chile, South America. There are tall cliffs where the desert reaches the ocean.

Fog forms at the coast and rolls inland across the desert. The water droplets in the fog are the only water that some desert animals have to drink.

The chinchilla eats roots, grasses and insects in the desert. These animals were hunted for their fur, and nearly died out. Now, farmers keep them on **ranches**.

A chinchilla has soft, grey fur.

People lived in the Atacama thousands of years ago. They found a **mineral** called copper in the rocks and made jewellery and ornaments with it.

This open-pit copper mine in the Atacama Desert is the largest in the world.

Today, copper is mined and sold to other countries. Some small towns grew up around the mines in the desert, but most people live near the coast.

The largest city on the coast is Antofagasta, in Chile. Ships carry the copper from here to countries all over the world.

The port at Antofagasta

# Glossary

**adapted:** if a plant or an animal can find everything it needs to live in a place, we say that it has adapted to that place. The animals can find food and shelter, and the plants have enough food in the soil and enough water. Some animals have changed their shape or their colour over a long time, so that they can catch food or hide easily. Some plants in dry areas can store water in their stems or roots.

**canyon:** a deep opening in the ground. There is often a river or stream at the bottom of a canyon.

**continent:** one of the seven large landmasses in the world. They are Europe, Asia, North America, South America, Australia, Antarctica and Africa.

**habitat:** the natural home of a plant or animal. Examples of habitats are wetlands, forests and grasslands.

**mineral:** something which is usually found in rocks. Metals such as gold, silver and copper are all minerals. They are mostly dug out of, or mined, from the ground.

**nectar:** a sweet liquid which plants make inside their flowers.

**nomads:** people who move around all the time rather than living in one place.

**oasis:** a place in a desert where there is water. The water may be in pools on the ground, or just below the ground. Plants such as date palms grow in oases.

**ranches:** large farms where cattle, sheep or other animals are reared.

**sand dunes:** mounds or small hills of sand made by the wind. They are found in deserts, and next to the sea.

**sand storms:** When the wind blows very hard over a sandy place, the sand is lifted off the ground and blown around. This is a sand storm. It is hard to see and to breathe in a sand storm.

**traders:** people who buy and sell, or exchange, goods.

**Tropics:** the parts of the world where the weather is mostly hot all year. These areas lie between the Tropic of Capricorn and the Tropic of Cancer. Lines on world maps and globes show where the Tropics are.

**wildlife reserves:** areas of land set aside for wildlife to live in.

# Index